GOSPEL AND CULTURE

GOSPEL AND CULTURES PAMPHLET 1

GOSPEL AND CULTURE

An Ongoing Discussion within the Ecumenical Movement

S. Wesley Ariarajah

WCC Publications, Geneva

Second printing: December 1995

Cover design: Edwin Hassink

ISNB 2-8254-1140-X

© 1994 WCC Publications, World Council of Churches,
150 route de Ferney, 1211 Geneva 2, Switzerland

No. 1 in the Gospel and Cultures series

Printed in Switzerland

Table of Contents

vii FOREWORD

x INTRODUCTION

1 1. GOSPEL AND RELIGIONS

18 2. CHURCH, WORLD AND KINGDOM

28 3. UNIVERSALITY AND PARTICULARITY

36 4. THEOLOGIES IN CONTEXT

46 5. THE CHURCH AND THE CHURCHES

51 6. THE TASK AHEAD

Foreword

At the heart of the Christian faith lies the affirmation that "the Word became flesh". This fundamental confession implies that the universal love of God, revealed in Jesus Christ through the power of the Spirit, manifests itself in particular contexts and through particular cultures. As the conference on world mission and evangelism in Bangkok (1973) put it, "culture shapes the human voice that answers the voice of Christ." The dynamic relationship between the gospel and culture, which "shapes" how humans understand, respond to and articulate God's revelation in Jesus Christ, has been a central issue in the life of the church throughout the centuries.

From the beginning of the ecumenical movement, the question of the relation between the particularity and universality of God's love and work in Jesus Christ has been on its agenda. The rich mosaic of member churches of the World Council of Churches is itself a constant and vivid illustration of how the gospel is lived through widely varying cultural expressions and in interaction with people of other living faiths. No wonder, then, that in almost every WCC assembly calls have been heard for a deeper theological study of culture and cultural plurality and a better understanding of the ways in which the gospel has interacted with cultures.

The central committee of the WCC has initiated a fresh and long-term study process on the relation between the gospel and cultures. "The ecumenical study process seeks to understand the implications of a gospel that both challenges and is challenged by the cultures in which it finds itself, in order that the churches and individual Christians may live and witness authentically" (WCC central committee, Johannesburg, January 1994). The study extends over a three-year period, leading up to the conference on world mission and evangelism in November-December 1996, whose theme is "Called to One Hope: The Gospel in Diverse Cultures".

One of the purposes of the study process is to encourage exploration of what has been the relation between the gospel and cultures in the history of the church and in selected areas around the world and to publish the results of such exploration in a series of pamphlets. It is hoped that these portrayals of the relation of the gospel to a culture in a given place will not only be informative to their readers in other parts of the world, but also provoke them to explore critically and creatively how culture shapes the understanding of the gospel and Christian life, spirituality and witness in their own context.

Wesley Ariarajah's is the first of these pamphlets. What better starting point than to explore ecumenical history so that the past may inspire and shed light on our present endeavour?

Within a brief compass, Ariarajah ably examines the concerns and content of the gospel and culture discussions in the history of the modern ecumenical movement and fruitfully identifies the central issues and main directions of the debates. While he does not discern any traceable "evolution" of the discussion on the subject within ecumenical history, he helpfully organizes the discussion around five central topics: gospel and religions; church, world and kingdom; universality and particularity; theologies in context; and the church and the churches. He then examines the background and presuppositions behind each of them and highlights a cluster of crucial issues and insights that have emerged.

Ariarajah's study rightly reminds us of the intrinsic relation between religion and culture. Encounter between the gospel and culture in many places is also an encounter between the gospel and other faiths. Therefore, the study of the relation between religion and culture is a continuing challenge even today. His study also draws attention to an urgent concern on the current ecumenical agenda, namely enabling various cultural expressions of Christian faith to be in dialogue with each other, thus bringing these diverse expressions into mutual accountability in Christ.

We live in a world torn between two opposite forces: a search for cultural roots and ethnic identities which is becoming increasingly separatist and destructive, and the forces of globalization which stifle struggles for the autonomy of the local and the particular. It is urgent in such a situation that churches commit themselves to a fresh exploration of the issues raised by the ecumenical movement in relation to the gospel and cultures. How pressing it is that, in the words of Philip Potter, churches everywhere participate together in God's work "in making the *oikoumene* an *oikos*, a home, a family of men and women... of varied gifts, cultures, possibilities, where openness, trust, love and justice reign".

As churches respond to the WCC's invitation "to explore afresh the relation between the gospel and cultures in their context and to take part in the study of this relationship", I am convinced this booklet will be immensely helpful. Those involved in the ecumenical study process on this topic owe a debt of gratitude to Wesley Ariarajah for this brief but significant introductory volume to a series of descriptive pamphlets. All who are participating in the ecumenical study of the theme — individuals as well as local study groups, research institutes and theological institutions — will find it valuable.

Christopher Duraisingh
Gospel and Cultures study
Programme Unit on Churches in Mission
World Council of Churches

Introduction

Controversy at Canberra

"Gentle but Radical" is the title of a video that draws a profile of Professor Chung Hyun-Kyung, one of the two speakers who introduced the main theme at the seventh assembly of the World Council of Churches in Canberra, Australia in 1991: "Come, Holy Spirit — Renew the Whole Creation". She was chosen as a speaker not because she was gentle or radical. The organizers were looking for two presenters — one from the Orthodox tradition, and the other, preferably a woman, from Asia, Africa or Latin America.

Professor Chung did more than what the organizers had hoped for. Approaching the theme as a Korean, as a woman and as a person from a culture that is predominantly shaped by Buddhism and Shamanism, she made a presentation which opened up yet again an issue that has often plagued the ecumenical movement and to which it has returned several times, the theme of "gospel and culture".

In the controversy that followed Professor Chung's presentation, she and many others challenged accusations of syncretism and compromise, and defended the right of people in all parts of the world and in all periods of time to explicate the meaning and message of the gospel. "Who has the right to decide that I am wrong, and on what basis?" This question was her basic line of defence. Do not Christians in every place and time have the responsibility to unfold the liberating message of the gospel in ways that make sense within their own cultural and religious milieu? Why is it wrong for women, freed from the inhibitions imposed by tradition, to articulate their experience of and encounter with the gospel in ways that are different from how it was expounded in patriarchal cultures? And how concerned should we be if the understanding of the gospel in one culture does not correspond to the way it was discerned and preached in another culture and at a different period of history?

Some of the participants at the assembly, however, were keen to emphasize the oneness and universality of the gospel message through time and space. There can be no "new" gospel for our present time, they argued; the only gospel is the one given to the apostles and handed down over the ages through the traditions of the church. The gospel can never be truly expounded outside the community of faith, which stands in continuity of shared truth through the ages.

While respecting the right of all Christians to seek to understand and expound the gospel in their own contexts, this group raised the issue of "limits to diversity". At what point, they asked, can we say that a particular understanding of the gospel is so far from the traditions of the church that it no longer stands within the Tradition of the one church?

Others challenged the very notion of "limits" to diversity. The Christian faith, they said, has only a centre — Jesus Christ — but no boundaries. There can be endless ways to appropriate the mystery of Christ, and no one interpretation of what God has done in Christ can fully exhaust its unfathomable riches.

The ecumenical debate during the assembly in Canberra and subsequently has reopened in a new way a question that was present at the very beginnings of the church and has often arisen in the ecumenical movement itself. The assembly and the central committee, which decide priorities for future WCC programmes, asked the WCC to take a fresh look at the issue of gospel and culture with the purpose of animating a new discussion in the member churches.

Several persons and groups have been approached to contribute to a broadly based four-year study of the issues involved, so that some tentative findings may be submitted for discussion at the next WCC assembly.

Facing new challenges

But the controversy at the Canberra assembly is not the only motivation for this study. There is a real need for a new discussion on gospel and culture today. For, when the gospel was taken to Asia, Africa, Latin America and the Pacific by Roman Catholic and Protestant missions in the 18th and 19th centuries, much of the evangelistic work was accompanied by colonization and Westernization of these parts of the world. The confidence which the colonizers had in the superiority of their own culture and religion led them in most cases to reject the culture of the people to whom the gospel was brought.

The devastating effects of this attitude on local cultures have been recalled recently during events that marked the 500th anniversary of the colonization of the Americas. Literature on this history abounds, and there is general recognition that the power relations between the colonizers and the colonized were at the heart of the indignity and rejection faced by peoples around the world. Some argue that these power relations are still at work today in the way we relate to one another's theology.

Several decades after the end of colonialism, churches that have emerged from Western missionary activities are beginning to look at what they have inherited as the gospel message and "Christian" culture. And they have a fuller awareness of the need to own the gospel anew in their own culture and in an idiom that makes sense to their own people. There is a new self-confidence on the part of those who do theology from various cultural perspectives as well as from the perspectives of women and the marginalized in society. At the same time there is a growing impatience with those who deny the legitimacy of this quest.

The ecumenical movement, which has encouraged and fostered these new developments, also has the responsibility to provide the forum in which Christians recognize one another as belonging to the one community despite the many new modes in which the gospel message is being understood and appropriated.

A second impulse comes from what is happening to and within Western culture itself, which has for centuries been the vehicle for the transplanting of the gospel message into different nations. Aspects of this culture and some of the theological traditions that have arisen from it seem to have strayed from the central message of the gospel. Many Christians who live within Western culture are uneasy about the ready identification made between Christianity and some of the social, economic and political systems that prevail within this culture. Some have pointed to the pre-Christian origins of many of the manifestations of this culture. Others are dismayed at its inability to challenge its peoples to Christian discipleship.

New and challenging questions are also being faced by Christians who live in lands where the gospel was first preached, and by churches in the Central and Eastern European nations that have been the home to some of the earliest traditions of the church. A rapidly changing political and social climate has raised new questions about the interpretation of the gospel to the world today. The experiences of churches of the Orthodox family, which have lived for centuries in close relation to the cultures of their people, have yet to be harvested and digested within the wider ecumenical discussions.

Again, the pressures of secularism, materialism and the growing technological culture, so pervasive in cities all over the world, raise issues in the area of gospel and culture that demand urgent attention.

All these developments provide the context for a new exploration of gospel and culture. But this booklet does not pretend to take on all these issues. Rather, it is an attempt to see how the gospel and culture discussions have been conducted within the history of the modern ecumenical movement, in order to uncover the different facets of the debates and the presuppositions that have governed the discussions. In examining the framework within which debates on this issue have taken place, we shall see how the historical period has to a large extent determined the main directions of the discussion. It is hoped that this study, by shedding some light on past discussions, will enable us to find an adequate new framework for our present endeavour.

The limitations

It is difficult to capture the discussions on gospel and culture within the ecumenical movement. The words "gospel" and "culture" are used in a variety of ways and there are no agreed definitions of them. Each discussion is based on an assumed definition or an implicit agreement about the sense of the words which often applies only to that particular discussion.

There is another serious limitation. This survey deals primarily with official meetings and statements. While these records and documents are important, they do not always reflect the rich variety of perspectives and positions taken in the discussions or the wealth of experiences and experiments in local situations that feed into them. Reflecting on this dilemma in response to an earlier draft of this booklet, Hans-Ruedi Weber said that "in ecumenical history the actual processes of thinking by persons and study groups reveal much more about the ecumenical movement than what drafting groups have written at conferences and assemblies".

This is particularly true of discussions on gospel and culture, for in such discussions people share far more of their own specific experiences in local situations than can ever be reflected in the final reports. This booklet, which deals with the broad outlines of the debate, is therefore meant to be complemented by others written by persons from different parts of the world who will deal with specific contexts and concrete issues that have been faced in trying to relate the gospel message to particular cultures.

There is no traceable "evolution" of the discussions on gospel and culture within ecumenical history. The historical moment, the challenges faced in the church's missionary task and the inner dynamics of ecumenical life, especially as more and more churches from Asia, Africa and Latin America have become active in the ecumenical fellowship, have influenced both the direction and content of the debates.

The issue is discussed here under five headings. There are, of course, other possible ways to approach the available material; and it is hoped that this booklet will serve as a resource and stimulus for the churches to take up this exploration and find their own ways to understand and assess what has gone on both in ecumenical history and in their own specific contexts.

The five topics which are the basis of the present study are:
— gospel and religions
— church, world, and kingdom
— universality and particularity
— theologies in context
— the church and the churches

These are not the actual topics under which discussions took place, and the concerns that arise under these headings overlap and inter-relate. The topics, however, as will be shown below, point to the various accents that have shaped the approach to gospel and culture in different periods of ecumenical history.

It is also important to note that the word "ecumenical" is used here in a rather narrow sense of the word. Normally the word denotes all the movements that contribute to the growing of the churches together into unity, mission and service to the world. Our discussion, however, is limited to the consideration of the issue within the modern missionary movement and the World Council of Churches. Useful discussions have taken place among other partners within the ecumenical fellowship, especially within the Roman Catholic Church after the Second Vatican Council (1962-1965). Those who wish a fuller picture should make a special effort to look up the developments there as well.

1. Gospel and Religions

Struggle in the New Testament church

The gospel and culture debate was already happening within the New Testament church and in the life and theology of the early church. The relationship between Jews and Gentiles and between Christianity and its Jewish heritage was a divisive issue in the emerging church. Whether Jewish law and practices should be maintained within the church was one of the major controversies among the apostles. Chapters 10 to 15 of the Acts of the Apostles record several incidents that throw light on this controversy; and the Council of Jerusalem relates the story of how the issue was temporarily resolved. Many of Paul's letters also struggle with the same concern.

Divergence within the early church

When Christianity eventually emerged as a Gentile church, its relationship to the philosophical traditions of the time engaged much of the attention of the theologians of the early church. The culture and philosophy of the Graeco-Roman world in which the church was taking root were to leave an indelible mark on Christian thinking. While polytheism and idol worship were rejected outright, the attitude to Greek culture and philosophy was more complex.

T.V. Philip, a church historian from India, has pointed out that there was no single line of thought within the early church. Tatian and Tertullian, for example, took a negative attitude to Greek philosophy. In an often-quoted statement Tertullian asked: "What has Athens to do with Jerusalem? What has the Academy to do with the church? We want no curious disputation after possessing Jesus Christ, no inquisition after receiving the gospel. When we believe, we desire no further belief" (*Prescription Against Heretics*, 7).

But Tertullian was fighting a losing battle. Several others were only too ready to adopt Greek culture and philosophy. Justin Martyr even defined Christianity as a school of philosophy. "Christ is the logos," he wrote, "of whom every race of men partakes, and those who live rationally are Christians even if thought to be atheists. Whatever things have been rightly said by any one belongs to us Christians" (*Second Apology*, 13).

Clement and Origen of Alexandria went much further, considering all wisdom to have been summed up in Christ, the uniting Principle. Both the Old Testament and Greek philosophy were seen as tutors to bring us to Christ, tributaries of the great river of Christianity. Clement described all history as one, insofar as all truth is one: "There is one river of truth; but many streams fall into it on this side and that" (*Stromata*, 1,5).[1]

A study of this early period would provide much illumination to a student on gospel and culture. However, this is beyond the scope of our present discussion.

The gospel and missions

During the early stages of the modern ecumenical movement it was usually the missionary imperative that provided the framework for the consideration of issues of gospel and culture. Mission organizations and individual missionaries realized that the gospel was being taken to people who lived according to different cultural traditions, and they were aware that those who took the gospel to other lands carried their own cultures with and in themselves. It is significant, however, that very little discussion took place in the early world mission conferences on the specific issue of gospel and culture.

Commemoration of the 500th anniversary of the colonization of the Americas, which led to the near elimination of indigenous cultures, and the story of the Aboriginal peoples of Australia, highlighted at the WCC's Canberra assembly, have brought a new awareness in the churches of the negative aspects of missionary expansion in close association with colonial expansion. Colonization, Westernization and evangelization were all characterized by an assumed superiority of what was brought to the religions and cultures of the peoples who were met and "conquered".

The ignorance, insensitivity and outright rejection of other cultures as "primitive", "pagan", "heathen" or "savage" has been well documented. But this is only one side of the story of the missionary engagement in other lands. In every country to which the missionary message was taken there are fascinating stories of individual missionaries who worked selflessly for the upliftment of peoples. Some laboured tirelessly to preserve local culture by committing ancient stories to writing and translating and making them known to the world. There were also missionaries and converts who tried to work out the meaning of the gospel in a specific culture. Often these attempts to indigenize the gospel took the form of adapting local customs, practices, festivals and dress, but there were also efforts to interpret the gospel within the thought-patterns or theological assumptions of other cultures.

In almost all early missionary debates, then, strong voices challenged insensitivity to other peoples and their traditions and appealed for a new look at the assumptions that undergirded the missionary enterprise. So it is indeed surprising that there is little or no specific discussion of gospel and culture in the reports of the early world mission conferences. Why was there no exploration of the meaning and significance of cultures that the missions met with? Was the missionary conscience not disturbed by the easy and outright rejection of the life of others as "pagan"? Why was an understanding of gospel and culture not at least a part of missionary strategy?

Focus on religions

Re-reading the records with such questions in mind, one is struck that the early missionary movement did not see the encounter of the gospel to be with the cultures of other peoples, but with their *religions*. Thus for the early missionary movement the issue was not one of "gospel and culture", but of "gospel and religious traditions".

J.H. Bavinck's statement that "culture is religion made visible" is perhaps the best summary of this attitude. The missionary movement believed that at the heart of every culture is a religion or a worldview that presents a general understanding of the nature of the universe and the place of the human being in it. It is religion that sets the standards of behaviour, the ethical judgements and the social interlinkages that hold communities together.

Culture, on this understanding, is only the working out of the central belief system in the day-to-day life of the people and in a social environment that sustains it. The missionary movement, therefore, was not enamoured of the heights of cultural achievement or the spiritual depth and beauty of a community's specific practices and modes of conduct. Since all these stem from religious beliefs, one must deal with the relationship of the gospel to the religion that is at the heart of culture, rather than with the cultural expression itself.

When we look at the problem from this perspective, we discover that the matter had indeed been a controversial issue within the early missionary movement. For already at the first world mission conference in Edinburgh (1910), as in all subsequent conferences, we encounter missionaries and others who called for a different approach to other religious traditions and, by implication, to other cultures.

A lengthy questionnaire, for example, was sent to missionaries in the field as part of the preparatory work of the Commission IV of the Edinburgh conference. Several of the missionaries responding to this enquiry spoke very highly of the ethical and moral values of people of other religious traditions. Many pointed to high spiritual attainments within the cultures of the peoples among whom they worked. They spoke of "points of contact" between Christianity and other religions and even of the enrichment to Christian faith that can result from a positive relationship to these religions.[2]

These conferences also witness to an emphasis on the need for humility on the part of those who bring the gospel to the nations. The importance of learning the local languages and practices was recognized. Missionaries were called to identify themselves with the people as Christ identified himself with the human community.

They were also encouraged to come to an informed understanding of the beliefs of others, not only to see the points of contact, but also to know what others actually believed. The world mission conference in Jerusalem in 1928 went even further to recognize the "values" in other faiths and call on all religious peoples to cooperate with Christians in resisting the evils of secularism, which was on the rise in the West and the East.[3]

But none of this led to a serious discussion on gospel and culture until after the third world mission conference in 1938 at Tambaram, India, because the missionary movement could not come to an agreement on the relationship of the gospel to religions. Even though from the beginning there were voices calling for "indigenization" or "inculturation" of the gospel, some with considerable passion, the missionary movement was reluctant to take this up for fear of syncretism and compromise with other religious belief systems. A discussion on "culture" as such had to await a changed attitude towards religious traditions.

Attitude to religions

The attitude to religion itself in the early discussions within the Protestant churches was influenced by two basic theological orientations: the Fall and Revelation.

The arguments ran along these lines: Since God created human beings in God's own image, one should expect human beings to share in the beauty and truth of God's own being. Human civilization could have reflected the glory of God. But the "fall", the deprivation that resulted from human sin, has completely eliminated this possibility. Since humans are basically sinful and in a state of rebellion against God (until they are reconciled to God in Christ), whatever comes from human efforts participates, in the final analysis, in human sin and self-centredness. Thus religion, even in its best and most elevated form, can be seen only as a merely human, sinful and vain attempt to reach God.

This understanding made a positive approach to religious traditions impossible. It reduced all religions, all beliefs and practices and all forms of religious life to a single level of activity that stems from and participates in human sinfulness. Since human beings cannot do good by their own effort, nor reach God by their good works, the only way they can have any knowledge of God is through God's own self-revelation. And the missionary movement was built on the belief that this divine self-revelation took place in the history of the people of Israel and has since been brought to its fullness in God's revelation in Jesus Christ. Only those who have encountered God in Jesus Christ can have a true knowledge of God and a life that flows out as a response to a relationship with God.

On the basis of these positive affirmations, several negative conclusions were drawn with regard to other religions. In so far as they are not based on God's self-revelation, religions are all too human. At best they can be indicators of the human longing for God, but more often they reflect human pride and rebellion against God in the very teaching that God can be known and grasped by human effort.

Whatever little hope might have existed in human development and progress was destroyed with the outbreak of war in Europe in 1914. The war confirmed the belief in the depravity of human beings in bondage to sin.

The theology of Karl Barth attempted to deal, out of the experience of the war, with the uncritical identification between gospel and culture, religion and state. Barth attempted to recover the prophetic dimension of the word of God and the challenge that the gospel brings to all situations. In so doing he made a radical separation between God's self-disclosure in the Bible, culminating in the gospel, and all forms of religious life, which were characterized as "unbelief".

Barth's theology had enormous influence on most ecumenical leaders of this period. It confirmed the basic attitude which considered all religions, including Christianity (as a religion), to be human attempts devoid of God's revelatory presence. The well-known Dutch missiologist Hendrik Kraemer applied this theological approach to mission. In his epoch-making preparatory volume for the 1938 world mission conference, *The Christian Message in a Non-Christian World*, Kraemer confirmed this basic suspicion of religions and the belief that the gospel is in "conflict" with them.

In arguing that there is a fundamental "discontinuity" between the gospel and religious traditions,[4] Kraemer challenged the attempts on the part of some of the missionaries and Christian thinkers in Asia who had begun to look at the gospel as the "fulfilment" of the longings of other religions. Kraemer argued that religions are "totalitarian systems", by which he meant that they are attempts to give a full, coherent and integrated view of life in its totality. They cannot be adapted partly or wholly in the service of understanding and responding to the gospel.

Kraemer was reacting not only to missionaries in Asia who were adopting new approaches to other faiths, but also to developments in the West, especially in the USA, where W.E. Hocking and others were calling for "a new alignment of religious forces" against the rise of secularism. Hocking's school of "liberal" thinkers were using the word "religion" to denote a reality that included different systems of religious thought which "merged in the universal human faith in the Divine Being". The leadership of the missionary movement saw this as a dangerous development, and Kraemer's theology sought to counter it.

Kraemer challenged

There were, of course, many voices from the East and West that challenged Kraemer's theology of religions. Some argued that God was present in a revealing way in other religious traditions. Others testified that they had witnessed among believers of other traditions lives that could only arise out of a living relationship to God. Still others doubted the application of the doctrine of the fall in so decisive a way as to eliminate the importance of human endeavour and spiritual achievements.[5]

The missionary movement on the whole, however, stayed with a theology that saw religions, in all their heights and depths, as no more than human attempts devoid of God's revelatory activity at best and, more often, in conflict with God's purposes for humankind. It was of course important to understand them, learn about them and respect them; for a missionary must be humble, sensitive and friendly to the people among whom he or she lives. But none of this meant that there is any "truth" in other belief systems.

When this attitude to religions is related to the conviction that all cultures are only expressions of religious systems, it is understandable that there were no separate discussions of gospel and culture in the early mission conferences. If all religions participate in error, it goes without saying that all cultures, which are further elaboration of religions, are also in error. Therefore, there was no room for the gospel to be "inculturated" or "indigenized". Persons of other faiths had to be called to leave both their religion *and* the culture which is the outward expression of that religion, in order to belong to an alternate community that comes out of the self-revelation of God in Jesus Christ — the church.

Thus peoples of other faiths in Asia, Africa or Latin America who respond to the gospel message should turn away not only from the religion that had shaped their life, but also from the culture that had nourished and is nourished by that faith. Although it was not required that the convert take on the culture of the person who brought the gospel, the fact is that human beings can only express their faith in a cultural milieu; and often this resulted in the convert's taking on the culture of the person who converted him or her to the "Christian way of life".

The radical change that takes place at the time of conversion was signified by the person's taking on a new name — often a biblical or Western one. Baptism was interpreted as the sign of belonging to a "new family". In extreme cases, the leaving behind of one's former religion and culture was signified by verbal renunciation or even symbolic acts like burning the scriptures or artifacts related to it.

Even though more dignified ways of renouncing one's former religion are in place today, much of the theology of religions that inspired the missionary movement and the attitude to cultures that emanated from it lingers on in traditional Protestant theology.

How then did discussions within the ecumenical movement move forward to such ideas as inculturation and indigenization? How did more positive approaches to cultures come about? Developments in world history provided the first impetus for the next stages of development.

National independence and the selfhood of the church

Six months after the conference in Tambaram, war broke out again in Europe. The "Tambaram debate" on religions was continued in Asia, but the European partners were engulfed by war. When the next world mission conference met, in Whitby, Canada, in July 1947, it was a different world — a world deeply divided and wounded by the ravages of war.

The United Nations had become a reality. Swift decolonization was to follow, first in Asia and then in other parts of the world. The urgency of responding to a world torn apart by war precipitated the formation of the World Council of Churches, which had been under discussion for some years. There was a new hope, however feeble, of a change in the power relations between nations and between churches.

The coming of national independence pushed Christians in many former colonies into a new self-awareness and a new relationship with peoples of other faiths, especially in the task of nation-building. This new reality produced the next stage for the debate on gospel and culture.

Already in Tambaram there was a new focus on the church, especially the local church, as the primary agent of mission. Much of the missionary expansion until that time had been spearheaded by foreign mission societies that were independent of the churches. But is not mission part of the life and rationale of the church? Does not the church in each of its local settings carry the responsibility for bringing the gospel to people among whom it is situated? Tambaram had clearly affirmed both the missionary nature of the church and its missionary obligation in its local context. This applied not only to churches that had existed for centuries but also to newly planted "younger churches" in all parts of the world. The younger churches must be enabled to discover and exercise their "selfhood".

When the churches in Asia and Africa themselves took up the issue of gospel and culture in this new mood of their own "selfhood", they were no longer speaking about "other cultures" but cultures of which they had been and were a part. The attainment of "selfhood" by the churches in every situation meant that they had to understand their own life and nature in the context of the culture in which they lived and to which they had to relate on a day-to-day basis. The foreignness of the churches in Asia and Africa and the accusation that they were the vestiges of colonial powers pushed these churches into a period of self-analysis and reconsideration of the assumptions of traditional Christian missions about relating to cultures. In no way could churches become partners in nation-building if they considered the religion and culture of the majority of the peoples with whom they lived to be in complete "discontinuity" with their new life in Christ.

New impetus from Asia and Africa

The first meeting of the newly formed East Asia Christian Conference (EACC) in Bangkok in 1949, therefore, claimed "that the Christian message may be made more challenging if it is presented in close relation to the special needs of the human situation in any given time, and also if it adopts and utilizes certain values in the traditional culture of each people". To this end, the statement went on to encourage the churches to "engage in a much more thorough study of the language, literature, music, art and social structure of *their peoples*, so that they may know more clearly where those are used, adapted or rejected for the service of the gospel".[6]

Here is a clear move away from the Tambaram position. There is no more hesitation based on the belief that culture is only the expression of the inner core of a belief system. While recognizing that some aspects of cultural expression may have to be rejected, the statement called on the churches to adopt and adapt those elements that can be of service to the gospel. It is significant that these cultures are no longer seen as those of "other peoples" but of "their peoples".

When the EACC met for its inaugural assembly in Kuala Lumpur in 1959, it had moved even further, arguing that "serious considerations should be given to indigenization, understood as relating the gospel to local culture, religious ideas and rapidly changing social situations". It called especially for "the indigenization of worship" and for studies of the social factors which tend to make a local congregation "a self-centred and inward looking group".[7]

A similar development was taking place in Africa, where the independent churches were beginning to see their own contribution to ecumenical life. The All Africa Conference of Churches (AACC) meeting in Ibadan in 1958 said that "while the church cannot give a Christian content to every African custom, we believe that the church throughout Africa has a very rich contribution to make to the life of the world church. Under God's guidance she will be enriched by the wealth which African culture can bring to her life."[8] The AACC's first assembly in Kampala made statements similar to the ones made by the EACC. "The church should study traditional African beliefs. Traditional African culture is not all bad; neither was everything good. As in all cultures, there were positive factors that held the culture together; there were negative factors which degraded human personality. The churches should become involved in a serious dialogue between the traditional worldview and the continuing revelation of Jesus Christ through the scriptures."[9]

The revolution had begun, and the floodgates were opened to a new assessment of the relationship of the gospel to the cultures of the peoples to whom it was taken. This also meant a re-examination of some of the earlier theological assumptions made within the missionary movement.

The 1964 EACC assembly in Bangkok urged that "the Christians of Asia must live more actually within the cultures of their own peoples. This may involve the abandoning of much that is familiar — a kind of self-emptying which will be both painful and dangerous. But it is only *so that the Spirit will show how the faith may be restated in the idiom of the indigenous cultures*, in forms of community life where the faith becomes luminous and in actions relevant to the needs of contemporary society." It went on to say that the churches are often afraid of achieving this selfhood since they have depended so long on missionary societies and missionaries and on "uncritical adherence to forms of organization and ways of behaviour devised during the period of dependence". [10]

The most striking image, popularized by Asian thinkers like D.T. Niles, was that of a potted plant. The gospel had been brought to the nations as a plant, with the pot being Western culture. This may have been inevitable. But now the plant must be transferred into Asian or African soil, so that it might strike deep roots and draw nourishment from it.

Thus, three factors — the independence of the nations that had been under colonial rule, recognition that missionary responsibility belongs to the church, especially the local church, and attempts by the "younger churches" to attain their selfhood — helped to shift the ecumenical debate on gospel and culture. This debate, however, was not an easy one within the missionary movement.

Culture reconsidered in the West

Even though the missionary movement had been silent about cultures in its early meetings, there was a prolonged debate already in 1928 at Jerusalem on the problems presented by the evolution of a "secular culture". Now with the new developments in the younger churches, the churches in the West were also ready for a new discussion of the issues.

It must be noted that the early hard-line position of "discontinuity" taken by Barth and Kraemer was conditioned by several developments. As we have already noted, attempts at an uncritical synthesis between Christianity and the religious traditions in some parts of Asia and voices within the liberal tradition in the USA which spoke of some form of universal religion caused considerable concern to the missionary movement. But more importantly, there was in Europe an unholy alliance between religion and culture which made it impossible for the gospel message to stand in opposition to and in judgement of activities done in the name of religion. Therefore in insisting that the gospel is in conflict with all religion, including Christianity, Barth liberated the gospel from its bondage to and close association with Western culture. In liberating the gospel from Christianity as a religious and cultural tradition of that time, Barth really opened the possibility of the free encounter of the gospel message with other religions and cultures.

Kraemer himself was a man of dialogue and was in a positive encounter with Islam and with Muslims during his years as a missionary in Indonesia. He too, like Barth, was keen to avoid mixing up the gospel with the negative aspects of the prevalent Western culture and was interested, in the first instance, to counter "liberal" thinking. But his application of Barth's theology to missiology, and especially to a theological assessment of other faiths, led him to the difficult concept of "discontinuity" between the gospel and religions.

Again, the insistence of Barth and Kraemer that God's self-disclosure takes place primarily in historical encounters did not help the discussions on gospel and religions or gospel and culture in the Asian and African contexts, where history is not perceived or experienced as the primary arena of relations between God and humanity. Barth's and Kraemer's views, however well-intended, were themselves very much culture- and history-bound. They resulted in a theological exclusivism that refused to take serious account of the religious experience within other faith traditions. Unfortunately, this thinking became the "main line" of Protestant missiology.

Recognizing this problem, both Barth and Kraemer began to modify their positions in relation to both religion and culture, especially in respect to other religions. Kraemer in his preface to *Religion and the Christian Faith* (1956) admitted that his Tambaram contribution had concentrated on non-Christian religions as human achievements and had failed to pay attention to the divine-human dialectic inherent in them. He turned to an analysis of human "religious consciousness" as a possible locus where God might be active. He even interpreted the post-colonial interfaith situation as paving the way for a "coming dialogue".

Nevertheless, these later writings did not succeed in changing the fundamental positions that had emerged within missions with regard to religions and therefore to other cultures. In any case, those who interpreted Barth and Kraemer for the missionary enterprise stayed with the hard line. It was Emil Brunner, another of the theologians who also had considerable influence on ecumenical thinking of this period, who picked up the subject of culture for a second look.

Brunner's contribution was to reintroduce the importance of culture to Western ecumenical thinking. He argued that, despite all the ambiguities, the close interrelation between religion and culture in all societies made the discussion important to the ecumenical movement. He saw several basic factors as going into the formation of culture. First there are purely natural factors, like climate, which shape cultural practices. Then there are the social and spiritual instruments human beings develop within a group and in a given geographical setting which contribute to the development of culture. Also part of a culture are spiritual presuppositions of a religious and ethical nature. Brunner went on to say that this aspect is not merely cultural, but can be considered as culture-transcendent presuppositions.

This was as far as Brunner was able to go in giving what might be called some "theological value" to other cultures. But he insisted that the character of truly human life in any culture can be created only by the Christian faith. In *Christianity and Civilization*, Brunner wrote: "In this book I seek to formulate and to justify my conviction that only Christianity is capable of furnishing the basis of a culturization which can rightly be described as human." He was convinced that all culture and religious life would come into a proper focus only within a personal and social existence determined by God's revelation in Jesus Christ and the faith that it creates.

Perhaps the best known study of gospel and culture within the ecumenical movement was the discussion by H. Richard Niebuhr in 1951 entitled *Christ and Culture*. In this classic book Niebuhr develops five conceptual models at work in shaping the approaches to Christ and culture:

— Christ against culture;
— the Christ of culture;
— Christ above culture;
— Christ and culture in paradox;
— Christ the transformer of culture.

After examining each of these positions, Niebuhr admits in a "Concluding Unscientific Postscript" that "our examination of the typical answers Christians have given to their enduring problem [of Christ and culture] is unconcluded and inconclusive". There were too many variants at work for him to take sides with any one of the models. Nor did he propose a model of his own.

The discussion of the issue of culture, therefore, moved forward not so much by a concentration on the theological meaning of culture but by important shifts that were to take place within the missionary movement in the understanding of the relations between the church, the world and the kingdom.

NOTES

[1] Cf. T.V. Philip, "Relation between Theology and Culture in the Perspective of Church History", paper given at the Taiwan Institute of Theology and Culture, January 1994.
[2] Sixty-one of the responses on Hinduism, for example, are available in typed form in the WCC library: *Commission on Missionary Message: Hinduism*, cat. no. 280, 215 W 893C, Vol. 2-3.
[3] *Jerusalem Meeting Report*, London, Oxford University Press, 1928, p.491.
[4] Hendrik Kraemer, *The Christian Message in a Non-Christian World*, London, Edinburgh House Press, 1938. For a summary and defence of his argument see Kraemer's contribution in *The Authority of Faith*: International Missionary Council Meeting at Tambaram, Madras, Dec. 12-29, 1938, London, Oxford University Press, 1939, pp.1ff.
[5] See contributions in *The Authority of Faith*.
[6] *The Christian Prospect in Eastern Asia*, Papers and minutes of the East Asia Christian Conference, Bangkok, Dec. 3-11, 1949, New York, Friendship Press, 1950, pp.118-119; emphasis added.
[7] *Witnesses Together*, Official report of the inaugural assembly of the East Asia Christian Conference, Kuala Lumpur, May 14-24, 1959, Rangoon, 1959, pp.109-110.
[8] *The Church in Changing Africa*, Report of the All Africa Church Conference, Ibadan, Nigeria, Jan. 10-19, 1958, New York, International Missionary Council, 1958, p.72.
[9] *Drumbeats from Kampala*, Report of the first assembly of the All Africa Conference of Churches, Kampala, April 20-30, 1963, London, Lutterworth Press, 1963, p.48.
[10] *The Christian Community within the Human Community*, Statement from the Bangkok assembly of the EACC, Feb.-March 1964, pp.15 and 52; emphasis added. The above citations are found in Ans J. van der Bent, "Christianity and Culture in the Ecumenical Movement", unpublished paper in the WCC archives.

2. Church, World and Kingdom

New developments in mission thinking

The rethinking of priorities following the war in Europe, the emergence of independent nations in the "mission fields" and the new self-confidence of the younger churches continued to influence developments within the missionary movement, as attested by the world mission conferences in Whitby, Canada (1947), Willingen, Germany (1952), and Accra, Ghana (1957). Not all of these are significant to our present discussion of gospel and culture, but it is important to note some of the general trends which contributed to changed attitudes in relation to cultures.

First is the concept of "partnership in mission". No longer was it possible to think of mission as going from one culture to other cultures or from one geographical area to all other areas. Since mission is the primary task of the church, churches in all parts of the world must enter into partnership with local churches in the exercise of their missionary obligation. This understanding led to the dwindling of the power of mission societies, which had until then dictated the theological basis for understanding and relating to cultures and religions in all contexts.

The second development is the emphasis placed on the "kingdom" and the "world" over against an excessive emphasis on the church as the focus of missionary thinking. While the role of the church in mission and the importance of the church as the koinonia of the believers in Christ was emphasized, the focus of the missionary activity itself looked more to the extension of God's sovereign rule over all of life rather than to winning converts to the membership of the church. At Willingen three significant mission thinkers of that period, Johannes Hoekendijk, Walter Freytag and Max A.C. Warren, challenged "church-centric missionary thinking" and called for an approach that began with the affirmation of the in-breaking of the kingdom in the world. This insistence that mission is a sensitive and total response to what God has done and is doing in the world provided a theological basis that was beginning to be more open to aspects in all cultures that were in concurrence with the values of the kingdom.

Willingen added to this the concept of *Missio Dei*, the "mission of God", of which the church's mission was but a part. It also highlighted the eschatological nature of the mission of the church: one engages in missionary activity with the conviction that it is God who will at the end gather up "all things" unto God's self. "All things" certainly pointed beyond the church. A serious attempt also was made during this period to give a stronger trinitarian basis for mission.

In essence there was a call for a reversal of the traditional direction of thinking, from terms of the church — the world — the kingdom to terms of the kingdom — the world — the church. Such ideas as the "world setting the agenda for the church" and doing theology with "the Bible in one hand and the newspaper in the other" were beginning to be aired. These bold new directions in mission thinking, which shifted the emphasis from the church to the world, raised questions that were to help further developments within the discussions on gospel and culture. Norman Goodall pointed to the unresolved questions raised by such directions when he asked: "What is the relationship between 'history' and 'salvation history', between God's activity in creation and his grace in redemption?"[1]

The call for a moratorium

Meanwhile, sharp criticism was coming from the newly emerging churches in the so-called third world of the history of the missionary movement's treatment of the peoples and cultures of which these churches were now more consciously a part. These sentiments were by no means new. Already at Edinburgh, V.S. Azariah of India, in what was considered a bold and daring speech for that period, had challenged the missionaries to become true fellow-workers with the local Christians. And Philip Ommen, general secretary of the national Christian council in India, had hinted in Tambaram that it was perhaps time for the missionaries to "go home" and leave the task to local churches.

Perhaps the most succinct summary of the new reaction to missions that were insensitive to local cultures is Emerito Nacpil's pithy statement: "missions but not missionaries". In a forthright challenge Nacpil, from the Philippines, called on the mission societies to leave the churches in Asia alone for some time so that they could discover themselves and their ministry to the peoples and cultures of Asia:

> This one final act of self-sacrifice on the part of modern missions is nothing less than the charter of freedom and life for the younger churches. In other words the most missionary service a missionary under the present system can do today in Asia is to go home! And the most free and vital and daring act the younger churches can do today is to stop asking for missionaries under the present system. And both actions — self-oblation on the part of missions and self-expression on the part of the younger churches — are consistent with the gospel by which they both live.[2]

A similar plea later by John Gatu of Kenya for a "moratorium" on Western missions in Africa also created quite a stir within the missionary movement.

The conferences in Willingen and especially in Ghana were preoccupied with the integration of the International Missionary Council with the WCC. When the WCC had come into existence in 1948, the IMC had decided to stay out so that association with larger concerns would not blunt its primary vocation of taking the gospel to all nations. The WCC and IMC, however, had cooperated on a study of the "Word of God and the Living Faith of

Men", which sought to explore some of the questions raised at the Tambaram meeting, the discussion of which was interrupted by the outbreak of war in Europe.

As the IMC looked to its integration with the WCC at the New Delhi assembly (1961), it had come a long way (as had the WCC) in its reconsideration of the issues of gospel and culture. This is evident in the report of the WCC central committee to the third assembly, which covers ecumenical developments from 1954-1961.

The report recalls the major study initiated at Willingen in 1952 to explore what it meant for churches in Asia, Africa and Latin America, which were brought into being by the Western missionary activity, to live today as local churches in "frontier" situations:

> What then does it really mean to be a Christian Asian or African today and to stand as such in his or her particular situation at this particular time? What is involved in being the local manifestation of the universal church within the context of present-day rapidly changing Asian or African society? What responses are Christian individuals and churches making to the varying pressures of their environment? How can they be helped to make a more effective witness, and what can all the churches learn from their distinctive experience?[3]

Although these questions are posed in the form of a general enquiry on the missionary obligation of these churches, another part of the report reveals its true intention: "The essence of this enquiry is to find out what happens as the young church reacts to pressures of the older traditional culture in which it is set, to the new impact of twentieth-century civilization and to the stresses and strains of rapid social change."[4]

In other words, the IMC and the WCC had launched through this study a new exploration of the question of the relationship of the gospel to religions and cultures, old and new. The findings of the study also witnessed to considerable struggle to discover a new basis for mission that did not arise from an outright rejection of other religions and cultures:

> The first stage of this enquiry led to the recognition of two important truths. The first was that the relationship between Christians non-Christians is based upon the sharing of a common humanity and on an equal place within the love of God. It is a human relationship founded not upon some meeting point of religious systems, but on the shared experience of secular community. The second was this: the gospel is addressed not to religions but to men and women. It seemed that at the point of the varying doctrines of man there might appear some mutual openness and therefore the possibility of vital encounter.[5]

This line of thought continues one of the strands that was also seen at the 1928 Jerusalem conference. The attempt is to separate the human person in his or her "need" from his or her religion and culture. The gospel, it is argued, addresses sinful men and women with the promise of new life. It does not address systems of thought. Such a position, however, proved to be unrealistic, for it was difficult to separate human beings from their beliefs and the culture that gives content to those beliefs.

In other parts of the report, therefore, this distinction is less obvious. For it also points to several subjects recommended for study by the Kuala Lumpur assembly of the EACC in 1959, which touched on both exploration of what Asian peoples of other faiths believed in a rapidly changing world and the need to revisit some traditional doctrines of the church on these matters. One suggested topic was "the significance of the eschatological view of the gospel and its relevance to hopes created by renascent Asian religions"; another called for a study on "the relation of the 'once-for-allness' of the redemptive act in Jesus Christ to God's concern for the redemption of men of other religions".[6]

Clearly, ecumenical thinking had come a long way since the Tambaram debate. Even though there was a concentration on "religions", their implications for our attitude to the cultures which come out of them were not lost sight of.

Study centres around the world were drafted into pursuing these questions from local perspectives. Several took up the challenge. A series of seminars organized by P.D. Devanandan and M.M. Thomas in Bangalore, India, attracted much attention. Devanandan popularized the idea that "creed", "cult" and "culture" are three concentric circles that influence each other. Even as the creed expresses itself in the cult and culture, there is also a reverse influence in which culture influences the cult and the creed. M.M. Thomas and Devanandan introduced into the debate several key concepts, such as "nation-building", "humanization of society" and "common humanity", which helped discussions on gospel and culture to move further.

The New Delhi report

The changes that had taken place in the Christian approach to other religions and cultures find explicit expression in the report of the WCC's New Delhi assembly. The importance of preaching the gospel and the belief that God saves all people through Christ are emphasized. But these beliefs are expressed within the wider perspective of God's relationship to the whole of humankind. The report honestly records also the disagreement among some participants about this view:

> Above all else, the Spirit stirs up the church to proclaim Christ as Lord and Saviour to all the nations and in all spheres of life. The church is sent, knowing that God has not left himself without witness even among men who do not yet know Christ, and knowing also that the reconciliation wrought through Christ embraces all creation and the whole

of mankind. We are aware that this great truth has deep implications when we go out to meet men of other faiths. But there are differences of opinion amongst us when we attempt to define the relation and response of such men to the activity of God amongst them. We are glad to note that the study of the question will be a main concern in the continuing study on "The Word of God and the Living Faiths of Men". We stress the urgency of this study.

Then comes this clear affirmation:

In the churches, we have but little understanding of the wisdom, love and power which God has given to men of other faiths and of no faith, or of the changes wrought in other faiths by their long encounter with Christianity. We must take up the conversation about Christ with them, *knowing that Christ addresses them through us and us through them.*[7]

The report of New Delhi's section on "Witness", in its subsection on "Communicating the Gospel", follows the same line. It claims that to communicate the gospel "involves the willingness and the ability of the evangelist to identify himself with those whom he addresses". It calls on the evangelist to "get alongside" the hearer and "to sit where he sits". This is an essential condition "upon which alone we may claim the right to be heard".[8] The evangelist must "share their concerns, sympathize with their aspirations and learn their language".

Also recognized is the cultural captivity of the evangelist: "It is Christ, not Christianity, which is to be proclaimed as the truth, as it is God's power and not ours which brings men to accept it."[9]

While the New Delhi assembly took up in its section on witness the emerging relationship with peoples who live by other religions and cultures and the implications of this for proclamation, there was a more considered discussion of culture itself in the section on service.

The report of this section begins with a clear statement striking at the root of any vestiges of the equation of Western culture with Christian culture. "A culture," it says, "is an integrated whole of ideas, traditions, institutions and customs, the setting of the life of a society, usually integrated around a religious faith." Having given this tentative definition of culture and acknowledging that "ours is world of many cultures", it goes on:

> The assumption that Western culture is *the* culture, and that therefore "Christian culture" is necessarily identified with the customs and traditions of Western civilization, is a hindrance to the spread of the gospel and a stumbling block to those of other traditions.[10]

The section report also recognizes that no culture is static. Cultures undergo change, although sometimes very slowly. But it argues that a culture is "an integrated whole" and that "the introduction of alien and un-assimilable elements too strong to be resisted leads to its collapse".

> Some of the conflicts of culture of our time were necessary, brought about by the unconscious, or by the well-intentioned but unthinking, imposition of Western customs and traditions... The great missionary movements of the church, however sympathetic and understanding of other cultural values, could not but lead to deep rooted clashes of loyalty.
> The cost of cultural conflict is high. We are not concerned with a cold appraisement of sociological trends. We are concerned with men and women, with the shattering of tribal loyalties and community customs, with the dissolution of age-old family patterns, with the aged, lost and bewildered in unfamiliar ways. The price is paid in loneliness and uprootedness. The tragedy is in the conflict between opposing ways of life, each of which is felt to be good.[11]

The section on culture also dealt with the problem of cross-cultural missions and more specifically the issue of gospel and culture. There was a recognition that the cultural disruption taking place was also a result of the imposition of science and technology. The report is clear, however, in rejecting a presentation of the gospel that would be disruptive of the culture of the people.

Towards the end, the report takes up the question of cultures in crisis and the disintegration of many cultures under the pressures and manipulations of modern media. Noting that in such situations new cultural life is sometimes organized around a new centre — such as a new ideology, religion or even political party — the report asks whether the Christian church could be "the nucleus around which will crystallize the culture of tomorrow". Reflecting on this idea, it proposes that at best Christian community — when it is rooted and grounded in Christ, serving him and through him loving God and neighbour — could function as "the leaven in the lump which lives and grows and gives life".[12]

The significance of New Delhi

We have spent considerable time on the period between 1948 and 1961, looking especially in some detail at the New Delhi report. That is because this was perhaps the most important period in the history of the modern missionary and ecumenical movement.

Until the Tambaram conference in 1938 the Western missionary societies more or less decided the meaning, method and consequences of Christian missions. It was they who played the major role in theological debates on the significance of other faiths and gospel and culture. The "younger churches" were still considered "mission fields". Often it was the foreign missionaries working in Asia, Africa, Latin America and the Pacific who spoke for and on behalf of these churches.

We have seen that there were a few notable exceptions, like Azariah and Chenchiah, who even at that early stage challenged the missionary conscience on how missions were conducted. But now the churches in the "mission field" were willing to speak for themselves. It should also be noted that New Delhi, meeting in the cultural context of Asia, was the first WCC assembly to be held outside the West.

The constituency and make-up of the WCC also underwent change at New Delhi. Most of the Eastern Orthodox churches that had hesitated to be part of the WCC in 1948 joined the Council at New Delhi. Also received into membership was a large number of churches from the third world. The WCC was becoming more truly a "world" council — with all the confessional and cultural diversity and consequences that would follow. And back in Europe, students and young people had already begun to rebel against the established culture and its hold on life.

NOTES

[1] Norman Goodall, ed., *Missions Under the Cross*, London, IMC, 1953, p.20.
[2] Emerito P. Nacpil, "Mission but not Missionaries", *International Review of Mission*, vol. LX, no. 239, July 1971, p.360.
[3] *Evanston to New Delhi, 1954-1961: Report of the Central Committee to the Third Assembly of the World Council of Churches*, WCC, Geneva, 1961, p.62.
[4] *Ibid.*, p.63.
[5] *Ibid.*, p.64.
[6] *Ibid.*, p.65.
[7] W.A. Visser 't Hooft, *New Delhi Speaks*, New York, Association Press, 1962, p.34; emphasis added.
[8] *Ibid.*, pp.35-36.
[9] *Ibid.*, p.38.
[10] *The New Delhi Report — The Third Assembly of the WCC*, London, SCM, 1962, p.98.
[11] *Ibid*.
[12] *Ibid.*, p.99.

3. Universality and Particularity

As the legitimacy of expressing the gospel in local cultures and the need to respect cultural plurality became more widely acknowledged, the ecumenical debate on culture entered a new phase, in which the focus was on the issue of universality and particularity.

What does it mean for a church to be part of a universal fellowship and confess a faith that is shared across nations and cultures and yet to be truly "local"? Can Christian faith in fact be expressed within the culture of each and every place? How can the gospel be both universal and contextual?

The following words from the report of the WCC's Uppsala assembly (1968), although said in the context of "The Quest for the Unity of the Whole Church", could equally have been said in the discussions during this period on gospel and culture:

> No church can properly avoid responsibility for the life of its own nation and culture. Yet if that should militate against fellowship with churches and Christians of other lands, then distortion has entered the church's life at a vital point. But the clearest obstacle to manifestation of the churches' universality is their inability to understand the measure in which they already belong together in one body.[1]

But how does this belonging to the one body relate to a people's own identity? What is the relationship of Christian identity to national and cultural identities? It is not without significance that the next world mission conference, in Bangkok in 1973, had as its topic for the work of one section "Culture and Identity". A central passage in the Bangkok report puts the problem in the following words:

> The problem of personal identity is closely related to the problems of cultural identity. "Culture shapes the human voice that answers the voice of Christ." Many Christians who have received the gospel through Western agents ask

the question "Is it really I who answers Christ? Is it not another person instead of me?" This points to the problem of so-called missionary alienation... The problem is: how can we ourselves be fully responsible when receiving salvation from Christ? How can we responsibly answer the voice of Christ instead of copying foreign models of conversion — imposed, not truly accepted?... The one faith must be made to be at home in every context and yet it can never be identical with it.[2]

Here the report seeks to deal with what was considered one of the central problems in the discussions of gospel and culture — the issue of identity. What makes a person Christian and what makes a person African? What does it mean to be an "African Christian"?

The Bangkok report goes on to tackle the problem of the universality and particularity of the Christian message. "Incarnation took place in a particular place in a particular context," it says. "Yet it has universal meaning: Jesus came to save the world." There is, according to those who drafted the statement, an analogy here to the problem of universality and particularity:

> The universality of the Christian faith does not contradict its particularity. Christ has to be responded to in a particular situation. Many people try to give universal validity to their particular response instead of acknowledging that the diversity of responses to Christ is essential precisely because they are related to particular situations and are thus relevant and complementary.[3]

This idea is then expanded by the claim that "proper theology includes reflection on the experience of the Christian community in a particular place, at a particular time".[4] And from this the report draws the inevitable conclusion that Christian theology by nature and necessity can only be "contextual". In fact the section had taken black theology as a test case to explore what a response to the message of Christ can mean in the context of racial oppression. The statement also goes on at some length to explore the issues of conversion and cultural change and the experience of women.

Explorations

The conviction that a genuine proclamation of the gospel must be contextual was also explored in different aspects of the programmes of the WCC during this period. The Bible provided some of the focus. From the beginning the translation of the Bible and the attempt to capture and convey its message in different languages and contexts had been one of the most challenging cross-cultural exercises. Translators had to enter the thought-patterns, images and symbol-systems of different cultures to be able to make the word once spoken speak again in a new context.

Within the WCC the desk on biblical studies specialized in conducting Bible study workshops in different parts of the world to explore and enable the reading of the Bible from within different contexts and cultural perspectives. The explication of the biblical message in Christian art in different cultures was unfolded in publications like *On a Friday Noon* and *Immanuel*, which show how the gospel has penetrated cultures at this level. Faith and Order studies of the authority of the Bible and its interpretation in the ecumenical movement also provided the forum for indirect and at times direct discussion of gospel and culture issues.[5]

The special study project on "The Common Christian Responsibility towards Areas of Rapid Social Change" and the *Humanum Studies* also touched on many aspects of the gospel and the emerging cultures. The latter included an "Enquiry into Indigenous Cultural Energies".[6]

The Faith and Order study "The Unity of the Church — Unity of Mankind" (later taken up as "Unity of the Church and the Renewal of Humankind") also attempted to tackle the problem of particularity and universality. One section at the Faith and Order commission meeting in Louvain (1971) was on "The Unity of the Church and Differences in Culture", but it could not go much further than identifying the areas that needed attention.[7]

Of greater significance in the work of the Faith and Order in this area were the worldwide studies and projects on "Giving an Account of the Hope that is in Us" and "The Community of Women and Men in the Church". These led to several publications that witnessed to the plurality of ways in which Christian faith is experienced and expressed in different cultural contexts.

Seeking community

By the time of the WCC's fifth assembly (Nairobi 1975), there was much experience to draw on. Furthermore, the gradual openness to other faiths and cultures that had begun with the study on the "Word of God and Living Faiths of Men" had borne visible fruits. This discussion, taken through several phases, had resulted in the formation in 1971 of the WCC subunit on Dialogue with People of Living Faiths and Ideologies. Though still controversial, the attitude of dialogue was gradually being accepted as an appropriate mode of relating to people of other faiths.

Significant changes had also taken place within the Roman Catholic Church through the Second Vatican Council. The Council had taken the renewal of liturgy as the first subject of discussion and promulgated in 1963 the first conciliar document on the sacred liturgy — *Sacrosanctum Concilium*. The celebration of the liturgy in local languages and the recommendation to adapt it to local situations opened up a whole process of officially supported indigenization and inculturation within the Roman Catholic Church. The Vatican II documents affirmed the importance of all cultures while maintaining that the gospel cannot be imprisoned in any one culture.

At the social and political levels, the period after the 1960s marked significant movements of social liberation, which led on the one hand to criticism of existing systems and on the other to cooperation across national and cultural lines in search of liberation from racism, sexism, classism and other oppressive structures. The intense search for community across barriers is mirrored in the title of one of the sections of the Nairobi assembly: "Seeking Community", which was defined as "the *common search* of peoples of various faiths, cultures and ideologies" (emphasis added).

The Nairobi assembly also reflected growing confessional and cultural diversity within the church. Meeting in Africa was a reminder of the sad history of missions and culture in Africa. And meeting at the height of East-West tensions urged the search for human community as a priority for the churches. The title of the assembly report, *Breaking Barriers*, said it all.

In dealing with plurality of cultures, Nairobi re-emphasized the need to keep universality and particularity in tension:

> The universal and the particular can oppose one another and can promote one another. Universality can grow out of openness to change and exchange among cultures. It grows also through the deepening of particularity which is received through increasing awareness of the distinct richness of one's own culture... In all this we recognize that varying cultures reflect the richness and diversity of humankind.[8]

While the changing characters of cultures and the dangers of "egoism reflected in cultural isolationism" were recognized, Nairobi's main emphasis was on cultural plurality as a blessing that should be preserved. In this mood it gave perhaps the most articulate rejection yet of the idea that some cultures may be closer to the gospel than others:

> Is there a specific Christian culture? The question is pertinent and loaded with the cultural imperialism associated with missionary history... Christian experience affirms that *no culture is closer to Jesus Christ than any other culture*. Jesus Christ restores what is truly human in any culture and frees us to be open to other cultures... He offers us liberation from attitudes of cultural superiority and from self-sufficiency. He unites us in a community which transcends any particular culture.[9]

The assembly further reiterated that the church must deal with its own cultural plurality in ways that build community, both within its own life and among others with whom it is called to live.

> As Christians with widely differing cultural history, we belong to that community which is the Body of Christ, the church. The church, too, should become embodied in every culture. It is called to fellowship in worship, freedom and service, sustained by a foretaste of God's kingdom. As such a community, the church is called to relate itself to any culture critically, creatively, redemptively. That means that within the Christian community each member should be open to the other, respecting the authenticity of his or her particular cultural form of obedience to the gospel, in the one church. Commitment to Jesus Christ takes different cultural forms. This is an expression of the church's catholicity.[10]

The Nairobi statement has been quoted in some detail here because it marks the culmination of a particular entry point into the gospel and culture debate. Subsequent WCC assemblies and world mission conferences have not been able to go much further on the specific topic of culture. The world mission conference in Melbourne (1980), for example, dealt with the issue of culture in two sections: "The Role of Churches in the Ongoing Search for Cultural Identity" and "Common Witness and Cultural Identity".[11]

Similarly the section on "Witnessing in a Divided World" at the Vancouver assembly (1983) had a sub-section on "Culture: the Context of our Witnessing".[12]

All point in the same general direction, affirming six major areas in which some consensus seemed to be emerging in ecumenical discussions:
a) the importance of the gospel's striking roots in each culture, expressed in life and worship that draws inspiration from that culture;
b) the recognition that the assumed natural relationship between Western culture and the gospel should be openly rejected;
c) the importance in all missionary work of being sensitive to the culture to which the message is taken;
d) the insistence that gospel does not take on everything in a culture, but also judges, transforms and changes cultural norms and practices;
e) the acknowledgement that culture is a changing reality and that one should be aware of the impact of the secular, materialistic and technological culture on all societies;
f) the need for Christians to respect the cultural plurality among themselves and to seek to learn from one another the different ways in which Christ has been accepted and acknowledged.

NOTES

[1] Norman Goodall, ed., *The Uppsala Report*, Geneva, WCC, 1968, p.17.
[2] *Bangkok Assembly 1973*, minutes and report of the assembly of the CWME, Geneva, WCC, 1973, p.73.
[3] *Ibid.*, p.74.
[4] *Ibid.*
[5] See Ellen Flesseman-van Leer, ed., *The Bible: Its Authority and Interpretation in the Ecumenical Movement*, Geneva, WCC, 1980. On the hermeneutical issues see the reports "The Significance of the Hermeneutical Problem for the Ecumenical Movement" (Bristol, 1967) and "Authority of the Bible" (Louvain, 1971).

[6] See Paul Abrecht's summary report of the study in *The Churches and Rapid Social Change*, New York, Doubleday, 1961, and David Jenkins, *The Humanum Studies 1969-1975, A Collection of Documents*, Geneva, WCC, 1975.
[7] *Faith and Order, Louvain 1971, Study Reports and Documents*, Faith and Order Paper no. 59, Geneva, WCC, 1971, p.193.
[8] David M. Paton, ed., *Breaking Barriers, Nairobi 1975*, official report of the fifth assembly, Geneva, WCC, London, SPCK, and Grand Rapids, Eerdmans, 1976, p.78.
[9] *Ibid.*, p.79; emphasis added.
[10] *Ibid*.
[11] *Your Kingdom Come — Mission Perspectives*, report on the world conference on mission and evangelism, Melbourne, 1980, Geneva, WCC, pp.182-83,200-201.
[12] David Gill, ed., *Gathered for Life*, official report of the sixth assembly, Vancouver, 1983, Geneva, WCC, and Grand Rapids, Eerdmans, 1983, pp.32-34.

4. Theologies in Context

The ecumenical discussion of gospel and culture has thus gradually moved to a different level since the 1970s. No longer was the question "What can we say about 'Christ and culture'?", but "How can Christ be confessed in different cultures?" "Confessing Christ" in several contexts became major programmatic focal points within the Christian Conference of Asia, the Lutheran World Federation and the WCC Faith and Order commission during this period. By the time of the Vancouver assembly, the overall encounter of the ecumenical fellowship had *itself* become more consciously, deliberately and openly an encounter of cultures.

What does this mean?
We have said that after the colonial period the churches, especially in former colonies, began to reflect on the meaning of being a church in their own context. This approach, over the decades, resulted in the development of new ways of understanding the meaning of the gospel, the nature of the church and the missionary mandate, which arose out of the experience of the churches in their local contexts.

Thus the churches in Latin America, reflecting on the meaning of the gospel in the context of poverty and oppression, developed theological methods that insisted on involvement and committed praxis as the starting point for all theological reflection. This led to a theological tradition that saw the gospel primarily as "Good News to the Poor".

The churches in Asia, living predominantly in the context of other living faiths, developed theological traditions that sought to re-evaluate the theological significance of religious plurality. They saw "dialogue" as the appropriate praxis from which theological reflection emerged.

Elsewhere in Asia, as in the Philippines and Korea, churches emphasized the experience of the people and sought to do theology that places the minjung (the suffering masses) as the subject of theological reflection.

In Africa, an intense search had begun to understand in greater depth the wisdom and vision of life that undergirds African traditional cultures.

In parts of the Western world there was an intense search for the "secular meaning of the gospel", in order to understand the significance of the gospel message for the "secular city".

The plurality of the theological quest was given further impetus as women reflected on their own experience and challenged the assumptions of the patriarchal culture on which traditional theology had been built.

Gradually, the issue of gospel and culture within the ecumenical movement had moved away from being a conceptual and practical problem in mission and into the arena of encounter among the theological traditions that have drawn their inspiration from the several contexts and cultures. The ecumenical movement itself had become, to borrow the title of a consultation organized in honour of Philip Potter, "a dialogue of cultures".

This dialogue, however, was not an easy one. The theological perspectives that emerged out of an ongoing dialogue with other faiths, for example, ran into serious difficulties at both the Nairobi and Canberra assemblies. Both the predominantly Western missionary theological tradition and some within the Orthodox theological tradition found it difficult to relate to a theology that sought to give theological significance to religious plurality.

Similarly, liberation theology from Latin America and feminist theology, which spoke out of the experience of women, also faced difficulties in establishing themselves as main theological streams within the life of the church.

The diversity of theological methods and reflections and the resulting difficulties in engaging in a common Christian theological discourse when churches met across cultures and contexts led the Vancouver assembly in its guidelines for WCC programmes to ask for reflection on "Vital and Coherent Theology" within the ecumenical fellowship.

Growing towards a vital and coherent theology did not mean that the diversity be minimized but that it be held together meaningfully for the enrichment of the whole movement:

> Growth towards vital and coherent theology should be one of the purposes of all programmes of the WCC. A vital theology will incorporate the rich diversity of theological approaches emerging out of the varied experiences throughout the world. A coherent theological approach will incorporate traditions and methods of reflection which represent the concrete needs and call of each and all members of the ecumenical movement towards unity of life and faith.[1]

This was further spelled out as the need for "interaction between the diversity of theological approaches" and for inter-relating the ongoing theological reflections on traditional theological issues such as "Baptism, Eucharist and Ministry" with "emerging studies of the relationship between culture, proclamation and unity and of the biblical and theological bases of social ethics; and encountering other faiths and modern ideologies".[2]

Recognizing that there is an intense search for new expressions of faith in concrete cultural situations, the Vancouver section report on "Witnessing in a Divided World" suggests that a conversation between the various cultural experiences of the gospel message may well form the "new ecumenical agenda" of the future:

> Therefore, in the search for a theological understanding of culture we are working towards a new ecumenical agenda in which various cultural expressions of the Christian faith may be in conversation with each other. In this encounter, the theology, missionary perspectives and historical experiences

of many churches, from the most diverse traditions (for example Orthodox and Roman Catholic Churches), offer fresh possibilities. So too do the contributions made by women and young people in the search for a new ecumenical agenda.[3]

The Vancouver report offered a useful summary of the steps to be taken in the study of gospel and culture, which incorporated the many elements of the debate thus far, namely, recognition of the cultural imperialism of the past, the issues of theological plurality as the gospel takes root in several cultures and the problems of cross-cultural mission. These concerns were summed up in five specific recommendations:

a) In the search for a theological understanding of culture, we can do the following: share a rich diversity of manifestations of the Christian faith; discover the unity that binds these together; and affirm together the Christological centre and trinitarian source of our faith in all its varied expressions.

b) We need to be aware of the possibility of our witness to the gospel becoming captive to any culture, recognizing the fact that all cultures are judged by the gospel.

c) In contemporary societies there is an evolution of a new culture due in part to modernization and technology. There is a search for a culture that will preserve human values and build community. We need to reassess the role played by, in particular, secular and religious ideologies in the formation of culture, and the relationship between the process and the demands of the gospel and our witness to it.

d) While we recognize the emergence of Christian communities within minority groups that affirm their cultural identity, we should pay special attention to the fact that many of these are in danger of being destroyed because they are seen as a threat to a dominant culture.

e) We need to look again at the whole matter of witnessing to the gospel across cultural boundaries, realizing that listening to and learning from the receptor culture is an essential part of the proclamation of the Christian message.[4]

The Vancouver recommendations, faithful as they are to the discussions held in this sub-section of the assembly, mark the beginning of the diversification of the agenda under the topic of gospel and culture.

For in addition to the primary problem of dialogue of theologies drawn from several cultural contexts, Vancouver had to deal with several threats to life which are the immediate result of the contemporary technological culture. The "culture of violence" that was so prevalent as the result of the growth of the military-industrial complex engaged the attention of the assembly. The materialistic consumer culture that was making inroads into all aspects of life and the resultant search for authentic spiritual life was of interest to others. There was even greater pressure from women to challenge the patriarchal culture of domination. Several other topics — the "culture of the poor and the oppressed", "the media culture", "alternate youth culture", "the secular culture" — were also raised as part of the conversations on culture.

While the main lines of the traditional debates on gospel and culture were narrowing into a discussion of "theologies in dialogue", contemporary problems had begun to impose themselves on the discussion.

The search for a framework

Within the WCC, the task of following up the Vancouver recommendations on gospel and culture fell on the Commission on World Mission and Evangelism, although it was decided that a group drawn from across all the programmes of the WCC should set the framework of the discussion, since gospel and culture was no longer seen as only a mission issue.

A consultation was called in Riano, Italy, in 1984 to define the scope of the study and its method. The multiplicity of concerns raised under the umbrella of gospel and culture at this meeting made it almost impossible to give a focus and set limits to the agenda for discussion. In fact, in attempting to set its focus, Riano went well beyond the recommendations from Vancouver to pick up several topics from much earlier discussions. It also lost the emphasis on the "dialogue of theologies" which Vancouver had recognized as a matter for urgent attention.

Riano identified five areas to be dealt with in a gospel and culture study process:

(i) *The theological understanding that undergirds the debates.* Is there anything we can define as a "pure gospel"? Is it possible to define culture? Is our understanding of the gospel inevitably affected by the cultural forms in which it reaches us, and how is it affected by our own cultural understanding?

(ii) *The meaning of evangelization.* There is much criticism of the cultural insensitivity of the modern mission movement. What, in the light of such critique, is valid evangelization today?

(iii) *Relations to other living religions.* The interaction, even identification, of religion and culture is obvious (India and Hinduism, Thailand and Buddhism, Iran and Islam, etc.). How do Christians approach such cultures, shaped by religious traditions different from Christianity? Is dialogue the answer; and if so, what kind of dialogue? What is the relationship of dialogue and mission? The problem of syncretism — is it a real problem?

(iv) *A re-look at Western culture(s).* Bishop Lesslie Newbigin speaks of the prime concern in mission of "the conversion of the pagan West". What is the prophetic stance of the gospel vis-a-vis Western cultures, especially dominated by Enlightenment models of thought, and where Westerners assume they live in a "Christian culture"? Can we disengage Christianity from Western culture?

(v) *How people at local levels can enter the discussion.* How to assist persons in local congregations, villages, rural areas, etc., to participate in this discussion, which has much impact on their lives.[5]

A study of the Riano recommendations highlights the tendency of gospel and culture discussions to run into the same traditional questions with little or no possibility of saying much more than what has been said before. Riano identified so many directions (many more, in fact, than the five listed above which were included in the report) that it was impossible to follow them up in a serious manner within the resources available to the WCC. It was felt that animating discussion of these issues in the churches at local levels might help to identify the priority concerns; and a consultation was held in Malaga, Spain, in 1987 to develop a study booklet to launch such an enquiry. The project, however, could not be implemented.

Despite the difficulties it encountered, the Riano meeting was able to comment on one important issue, namely that of "criteria". Gospel and culture debates had often been paralyzed by the issue of finding "gospel criteria" to judge cultures. Riano made a firm statement on the difficulties that attend this attempt. In so doing, it also indirectly hinted that the emergence of theological traditions out of an encounter with cultures is, as Vancouver had suggested, the proper focus of the discussions:

> We attempted to single out certain gospel criteria for evaluating cultures. There are identifiable signs of the gospel wherever the fullness of life is granted to all people, especially the poor and marginalized, and wherever love, freedom and justice are experienced in the light of the cross and resurrection. *However, we doubt whether it is possible and proper to the incarnational approach to sort out gospel*

criteria for evaluating cultures. If we take seriously the theological assumption of the gospel transforming cultures from within, and if the gospel cannot be considered independent from its various cultural expressions, how can we single out universally applicable gospel criteria?[6]

The five-point agenda for study set up by Riano could not be followed up. One of the reasons for this was precisely the diversity of theological methods and perceptions present within the group that sought to set up the study.

So when the next world mission conference met in San Antonio, Texas, in 1989 the director of the Commission on World Mission and Evangelism, who had struggled very hard to get the programme going at Riano and Malaga, admitted in his report that "it is easier to note the crucial importance of the relationship of gospel and culture than it is to suggest ways to secure a creative interrelationship of the two".[7]

His own suggestions of what needed to be done showed how far the discussion had strayed since Vancouver. He saw the need:

1) to challenge the strong impact of secularistic, technological, consumerist and often militarist cultures that spread across the globe, frequently masquerading as "Christian", and
2) to seek to affirm the many cultures of the poor who, often in suffering, evidence marks of grace and beauty that are surely gifts of the Spirit.

He insisted in addition that a "profound understanding of the relationship of the Christian gospel and culture should lead us towards greater justice for women in both society and the church".[8]

The San Antonio conference had no specific group working on gospel and culture. "It was decided, rightly or wrongly, not to do that, but rather to recognize that gospel and culture permeate the work of every section of the conference". All four section reports of San Antonio, therefore, took up the question of culture in different ways:

Section I, "Turning to the Living God", dealt specifically with the issues of witnessing to the gospel in a secular society and among people of living faiths. In both these areas, as well as in the sub-section on "Communicating the Gospel Today", the emphasis was on cultural sensitivity and openness to what God is doing among the peoples to whom the gospel is taken.

Section II, "Participating in Suffering and Struggle", went into a more substantial discussion on "the power of culture and community":

> Each community has a culture — by which is meant the totality of what constitutes its life, all that is essential for relationships among its members, and its relationship with God and with the natural environment. It is in relation to community that people define their identity. Community and culture are inter-related as body and soul. The cultural dynamics is manifested in the daily life of the community and in each of its members.[9]

At the same time the report warns that culture and community may also "be absolutized and then power misused to exclude and oppress other people". It recalls several instances in which the culture and community of indigenous peoples have been destroyed and suppressed in the name of community and culture.

The theme is also taken up in Section III on "The Earth is the Lord's", whose report gives several concrete examples of the many functions of culture in human communities. Special mention is made of how different cultures relate to the stewardship of the earth.

In Section IV on "Renewed Communities in Mission", San Antonio takes up the question of criteria and cultural sensitivities in cross-cultural missions.

An overall assessment of the period following Vancouver shows that the WCC had considerable difficulty in dealing with the issue of gospel and culture. The discussions have been repetitive, going around in circles and taking both an affirmative and cautionary approach to culture. The difficulty also lies in the formulation gospel *and* culture, which implies that there is a gospel which is "culture-free" and that cultures are devoid of gospel values until in some sense transformed by it.

Vancouver was able to discern that the discussion had to be moved to the level of the different ways in which the gospel had in fact made sense in different cultural contexts. But, as we have seen, the plurality of interests in the study in the post-Vancouver period unfortunately drew the discussion away from this primary focus, with the result that new impetus for the discussion did not come either from the WCC's work or the San Antonio meeting; and the report of the Programme Policy Committee at the seventh assembly in Canberra (1991) had to acknowledge with regret "that there is no substantive report on the basis of which to evaluate how we have grown in the area of gospel and culture".[10]

NOTES

[1] Gill, ed., *Gathered for Life*, p.251.
[2] *Ibid.*, p.254.
[3] *Ibid.*, p.33.
[4] *Ibid.*, pp.33-34.
[5] Eugene L. Stockwell, "Gospel and Culture in the Ecumenical Debate", unpublished paper, January 1988, WCC archives.
[6] *Ibid.*, p.3; emphasis added.
[7] Frederick R. Wilson, *The San Antonio Report: Your Will Be Done — Mission in Christ's Way*, Geneva, WCC, 1990, p.123.
[8] *Ibid.*
[9] *Ibid.*, p.43.
[10] Michael Kinnamon, ed., *Signs of the Spirit*, official report of the seventh assembly, Canberra, 1991, Geneva, WCC, 1991, pp.183-84.

5. *The Church and the Churches*

The theme for the WCC's seventh assembly in Canberra in 1991 centred on the Holy Spirit, "Come, Holy Spirit — Renew the Whole Creation", unlike most of the earlier assemblies, whose themes were Christocentric. It was hoped that this pneumatological emphasis and the focus on the renewal of the "whole creation" would open up several new entry points to some of the classical discussions within the ecumenical movement.

The organizers, however, had not planned a substantive discussion on gospel and culture within the formal agenda of the assembly. The question, however, surfaced as one of the two major controversial issues (the other was the Gulf war) to engage the assembly's attention.

The issue of gospel and culture became part of the assembly's life as the result of two presentations which were different yet interrelated. The first was the presentation by the Aborigines of Australia, whose culture had been at the receiving end of the negative aspects of the missionary movement. In a moving and powerful presentation the Aborigines recalled the story of the colonization of Australia, which resulted in virtual genocide of the first peoples of the land. They showed how those who presented the gospel completely rejected and disregarded the cultural and spiritual heritage of aboriginal peoples.

It is important to note that the physical presence and the direct challenge issued by the first peoples of Australia made gospel and culture at the seventh assembly a living reality that had to be encountered, not just another intellectual issue to be discussed. The Aboriginal peoples, for example, held a traditional ceremony to give permission to the WCC general secretary to hold the assembly on their land. The ceremony, held in the worship tent, was preceded by an invitation to all participants to pass through smoke (from burning green leaves) as a sign of purification for worship. As Aborigines danced in traditional costume around the altar and invited people to pass through smoke, much that would have been rejected outright as "paganism" in an earlier period was being presented to some four thousand people gathered from all Christian confessions and cultures as authentic Christian practice. The explanations were given by an Aboriginal Anglican bishop, Arthur Malcolm.

Before, during and after the assembly several people found it difficult to accept aspects of the Aboriginal presentations as integral to the Christian faith they confessed. Some were shocked and could not see themselves as part of the church presented there. Many others remained silent, attempting to understand the full implications of the event to their understanding of the faith.

The Aboriginal presence and participation thus brought the world church in confrontation with the gospel and culture issue through the eyes of an ancient culture.

The second presentation was the controversial one mentioned earlier, by Chung Hyun-Kyung, who challenged the assembly by relating the gospel to contemporary attempts to understand the faith in context.

"I would like to invite all of you", she said in her opening presentation on the theme, "to get on the holy ground with me by taking off your shoes while we are dancing to prepare the way of the Spirit. With humble heart and body let us listen to the cries of creation and the cries of the Spirit within it." Her "cries of the Spirit" included not only "the spirit of Hagar, Egyptian black slave woman exploited and abandoned by Abraham and Sarah, the ancestors of our faith...", but also "the spirit of people killed in Hiroshima and Nagasaki..., the spirit of Mahatma Gandhi, Steve Biko, Martin Luther King Jr., Malcolm X..., the spirit of the Amazon rain forest..., and of earth, air and water, raped, tortured and exploited by human greed for money..."

Professor Chung expounded the interconnections brought by the Spirit by referring to *ki*, the life energy, the breath and the wind of life in traditional North East Asian thinking, and saw in the image of the woman Buddhist *bodhisattva* Kwan In the compassion and self-giving love on the cross.[1]

Her presentation accompanied one by Patriarch Parthenios of Alexandria and All Africa, who also offered a thought-provoking exploration of the theme, though from within the more familiar language and traditions of the church. It is fascinating, from both a theological and a gospel and culture perspective, to do a comparative study of the two presentations.

Chung's presentation, however, raised considerable controversy. Some were fascinated by what they had heard, seeing it as an authentic exposition of the meaning of the Spirit which was both contemporary and contextual. Others accused her of syncretism. To them her presentation appeared to have over-stepped the limits of contextual theology.

The strongest statement came from an Orthodox reflection presented to the Assembly, which expressed nervousness both on the area of relations with other faiths and on contextualization of theology:

> The Orthodox support dialogue initiatives, particularly those aiming at the promotion of relations of openness, mutual respect and human cooperation with neighbours of other faiths. When dialogue takes place, Christians are called to bear witness to the integrity of their faith... All this, however, must occur on the basis of theological criteria which will define the limits of diversity. The biblical faith in God must not be changed.[2]

On the specific presentation of Professor Chung the Orthodox said:

> The Orthodox wish to stress the factor of sin and error which exists in every human action, and separate the Holy Spirit from these. We must guard against a tendency to substitute a

> *"private" spirit, the spirit of the world or other spirits for the Holy Spirit* who proceeds from the Father and rests in the Son. Our tradition is rich in respect for local and national cultures, but we find it impossible to evoke the spirits of "earth, air, water and sea creatures". Pneumatology is inseparable from Christology or from the doctrine of the Holy Spirit confessed by the church on the basis of divine revelation.[3]

The Orthodox were by no means the only group to express theological reservations about Chung's presentation. Many others had a difficult task assimilating the unfamiliar approach to what they had believed in their contexts.

It is not the theological "correctness" or otherwise of the presentation that is at issue here. The most important aspect of the many-sided debate that followed was the clear insistence by both the Aboriginal peoples and Professor Chung that they were explicating nothing other than the one gospel and are therefore speaking from within the church. Some of the Orthodox and other participants, however, saw little continuity in content with the traditional way of presenting the Christian message. They therefore pointed to the need for setting "limits to diversity".

Did everyone there belong to the one church, and were they able to recognize one another as sisters and brothers in Christ? And who has the authority to say that a particular understanding and presentation of the gospel was beyond the bounds of acceptability?

The Canberra debate has brought a renewed urgency into the ecumenical exploration of gospel and culture, pointing to the need to find a new framework for the discussion in the future. What are the essential marks of a Christian and of the church in any culture? And how can Christians who can and must interpret the gospel in their own culture recognize others in other cultures as belonging to the one family in Christ? Are there real limits to diversity, or is there only a centre for the faith, and everything that comes out of and relates to that centre is a valid expression of the faith? What are the power elements at play here? For who, in the ecumenical context, has the teaching authority to say that a particular interpretation or response to the gospel in a given culture puts a person or a community outside the bounds of the church?

In other words, at Canberra, the gospel and culture issue moved from being only a question of "theologies in dialogue" into an ecclesiological issue as well — of the church and the churches in the context of cultural plurality.

NOTES

[1] Kinnamon, ed., *Signs of the Spirit*, pp.37-46.
[2] *Ibid.*, p.280.
[3] *Ibid.*, p.281.

6. *The Task Ahead*

Thus at the end of the seventh assembly we are left once again with a major study on gospel and culture. The WCC's Programme Unit II, Churches in Mission, has the responsibility to follow up this study. As indicated in the introduction, it has laid out a four-year study programme enabling the issue to be taken up in every region of the world. An effort will be made to facilitate a study of the historical processes of the encounter between the gospel and specific cultures in the regions. Small groups will also be formed in several places to explore the meaning of the gospel in specific cultural contexts.

It is hoped that this process will lead to several regional meetings, which will eventually feed into the next world mission conference in November 1996. It is also hoped that the outcome of the dialogue at the world mission conference will form the basis for a presentation to the WCC's eighth assembly in 1998.

This brief and in many ways sketchy history of the discussions within one part of the ecumenical fellowship is presented here in the hope that it will assist, as we look forward to this study in all the regions, in avoiding the familiar pitfalls, in building on the past and also in finding imaginative new ways of approaching the issue. It is also offered in the hope that interested readers will go to the sources identified and do their own reading of the events and developments. There are certainly many ways to read and interpret this complex and fascinating story.